# Weird Animal Diets
# Poop-Eating Animals

by Libby Wilson

FOCUS READERS.

BEACON

# www.focusreaders.com

Focus Readers is distributed by North Star Editions:
sales@northstareditions.com | 888-417-0195

Produced for Focus Readers by Red Line Editorial.

Photographs ©: Shutterstock Images, cover, 1, 4, 6, 8, 11, 13, 14–15, 16, 19, 21, 22, 25, 27, 29

**Library of Congress Cataloging-in-Publication Data**
Names: Wilson, Libby, author.
Title: Poop-eating animals / by Libby Wilson.
Description: Lake Elmo, MN : Focus Readers, [2022] | Series: Weird animal diets | Includes index. | Audience: Grades 2-3
Identifiers: LCCN 2021033824 (print) | LCCN 2021033825 (ebook) | ISBN 9781637390542 (hardcover) | ISBN 9781637391082 (paperback) | ISBN 9781637391624 (ebook) | ISBN 9781637392126 (pdf)
Subjects: LCSH: Animals--Food--Juvenile literature. | Animal droppings--Juvenile literature. | Animal behavior--Juvenile literature.
Classification: LCC QL756.5 .W56 2022  (print) | LCC QL756.5  (ebook) | DDC 591.5--dc23
LC record available at https://lccn.loc.gov/2021033824
LC ebook record available at https://lccn.loc.gov/2021033825

Printed in the United States of America
Mankato, MN
012022

# About the Author

Libby Wilson is a retired elementary librarian who has always loved reading and writing stories. She would like to thank Michael Gardner, Associate Professor at Flinders University in Australia, who helped locate scientific studies for this book. She also thanks Sloane and Harvey Wilson for the sloth moth idea.

# Table of Contents

# Chapter 1

# A Natural Food

An Egyptian vulture soars above a mountain. He spots a goat. Down he swoops. The vulture lands. He searches along the ground. He finds what he came for. It's goat poop! The vulture begins eating.

 **Egyptian vultures sometimes eat the poop of animals such as cows, sheep, and goats.**

 **Egyptian vultures eat dead animals as well as rotting fruits and vegetables.**

Goat poop has a certain **nutrient**. It turns the vulture's face yellow. Scientists think the color tells other vultures he is strong. A yellow face may also help him find a mate.

Getting nutrients is one of many reasons animals eat poop. Eating poop is a common and natural act for many animals. It keeps them healthy and safe. Animal poop is an important part of the **food chain**. Some animals might not survive without it.

**Did You Know?**

Eating even a bit of poop can make people sick. A speck of poop can contain billions of germs.

# Chapter 2

# Eating Poop for Gut Bacteria

Pandas eat mostly bamboo. Bamboo stems have lots of **fiber**. The fiber makes bamboo hard to **digest**. But pandas have certain **bacteria** in their guts. The bacteria break down the fiber.

 Pandas must spend 10 to 16 hours each day eating to get all the food they need.

Panda cubs are born without the bacteria. This means they can't digest bamboo. Without bamboo, cubs won't grow well. So, cubs eat their mothers' poop. It fills their guts with good bacteria. Then they can digest bamboo.

Similarly, koala babies cannot digest leaves at first. Newborn koalas stay inside their mother's pouch. They drink her milk. After six months, they climb outside. They eat their mother's poop. Then

 **A koala baby is called a joey. A joey peeks out from its mother's pouch.**

the babies can eat leaves. The poop's bacteria help them digest the leaves.

In fact, many **herbivore** babies must eat their parents' poop. This is true for elephants and hippos.

It's true for horses and pigs, too. The plants they eat are hard to digest. First, babies drink their mother's milk. Next, they eat their parents' poop to get gut bacteria. Then, the babies can eat plants.

Termites eat mostly wood. Wood is very hard to digest. So, newly

**Did You Know?**

Scientists found a baby mammoth that had been frozen for 42,000 years. The mammoth had her mother's poop in her stomach.

 **Thanks to their gut bacteria, termites can feast on rotting wood.**

hatched termites must eat the poop of adult termites to get gut bacteria. Also, termites change forms many times during their lives. To get new gut bacteria, they must eat poop every time they change.

# Rabbits

Rabbits have two kinds of poop. One kind is a hard fiber pellet. Rabbits leave this poop on the ground. The other kind is a soft, sticky pellet. It's filled with good bacteria and partly digested food.

A rabbit bites off this soft pellet as it leaves the rabbit's body. Then the rabbit eats it. The food passes through the rabbit again. This time, the rabbit can fully digest it. The rabbit gets the nutrients it needs to be healthy.

Hard pellets are mostly fiber that rabbits can't digest.

# Chapter 3

# Eating Poop for Nutrients

Warthogs are African herbivores. They are grazers. They eat mostly grasses. But sometimes they eat elephant poop. Elephant poop contains a lot of food. Elephants eat grasses, leaves, and branches.

 **Warthogs kneel on their front legs to find food close to the ground.**

These foods are hard to digest. So, an elephant's food often comes out looking much like it did on the way in.

Also, elephants eat high tree branches and leaves. Warthogs can't reach this food. But elephants poop it out. Warthogs get the food's nutrients by eating the poop.

**Did You Know?**

Elephants digest only about half of what they eat.

 **Elephant poop has many nutrients that other animals can eat.**

Through pooping, tall animals bring nutrients to ground level.

Some gorillas eat their own poop during fruit season. They eat fruit seeds to get important **protein**.

But the seeds are too hard to digest. So, gorillas poop out the seeds and eat them again. This time, they can digest the nutrients.

Some African tortoises need a lot of fiber. They usually get the fiber from plants. But in dry times, few plants grow. So, tortoises eat rabbit fiber pellets. The pellets can make up one-fourth of the tortoises' diet.

Certain moths live in the fur of tree sloths. Once a week, sloths climb down the trees to poop. The

 **Sloths take a long time to digest their food. So, they need to poop only once a week.**

moths lay eggs in the poop. Newly hatched moths eat the poop for nutrients. Then the young moths grow wings. They fly up and live in the sloths' fur.

# Chapter 4

# Eating Poop for Safety

Each animal's poop has its own odor. Just by the smell, animals can tell who is nearby. Baby animals can be an easy meal. So, predators smell for baby animals' poop.

 **If predators can smell the poop of their prey, the prey is likely nearby.**

But mother deer will eat their fawns' poop. Songbirds will eat their nestlings' poop. This keeps predators from finding their babies.

Wolves usually poop outside their den. But cubs and sick wolves may poop inside. This poop is eaten right away. The poop may contain harmful **parasite** eggs. The eggs would hatch in a few days. The parasites could sicken the whole den. Eating the poop keeps the den clean and keeps the wolves healthy.

 **Wolves poop outside the den to keep the den clean.**

Young dung beetles grow up safely inside poop. Adult beetles form a ball from herbivore poop.

They push hard to roll the ball to a safe spot. Next, they bury it. The female lays one egg inside the ball. The egg hatches. The young beetle eats the poop around it. It emerges when it is fully grown.

Dung beetles recycle poop. They push it underground. The poop's nutrients **enrich** the soil. Then, new

**Did You Know?**

Dung beetles can move dung balls 50 times their own weight.

 **A dung beetle rolls poop into a ball.**

life can grow. Dung beetles and
other poop-eating animals clean
up piles of germ-filled poop. Their
poop-eating creates a healthier,
safer Earth.

# FOCUS ON
# Poop-Eating Animals

*Write your answers on a separate piece of paper.*

**1.** Write a paragraph summarizing how eating poop keeps animals healthy and safe.

**2.** Would you want to have a pet that is a poop-eater? Why or why not?

**3.** Why do mother deer eat their fawns' poop?
- **A.** to get gut bacteria to help them digest
- **B.** to hide their babies from predators
- **C.** to get protein and nutrients

**4.** What would happen if baby koalas did not eat their mother's poop?
- **A.** The babies would not get enough nutrients.
- **B.** The babies would eat leaves right away.
- **C.** The babies would leave their mother's pouch more quickly.

**5.** What does **emerges** mean in this book?

*The female lays one egg inside the ball. The egg hatches. The young beetle eats the poop around it. It **emerges** when it is fully grown.*

    **A.** lays an egg

    **B.** eats a lot

    **C.** comes out

**6.** What does **nestlings** mean in this book?

*Songbirds will eat their **nestlings'** poop. This keeps predators from finding their babies.*

    **A.** animals that eat birds

    **B.** food for birds

    **C.** baby birds

*Answer key on page 32.*

# Glossary

**bacteria**
Tiny living things that can be either useful or harmful.

**digest**
To break down food so it can be used by the body.

**enrich**
To increase the quality or value of something.

**fiber**
The tough parts of plants that are hard for the body to break down.

**food chain**
The feeding relationships among different living things.

**herbivore**
An animal that eats mostly plants.

**nutrient**
A substance that living things need to stay strong and healthy.

**parasite**
An animal or plant that lives on or in another living thing.

**protein**
A substance in the body that tells a living cell what to do.

# To Learn More

## BOOKS

Duhig, Holly. *Barf and Poop*. Minneapolis: Lerner Publications, 2020.

Montgomery, Heather L. *Who Gives a Poop?* New York: Bloomsbury, 2020.

Stewart, Melissa. *Ick! Delightfully Disgusting Animal Dinners, Dwellings, and Defenses*. Washington, DC: National Geographic Kids, 2020.

## NOTE TO EDUCATORS

Visit **www.focusreaders.com** to find lesson plans, activities, links, and other resources related to this title.

# Index

## A
African tortoises, 20

## B
bacteria, 9–13, 14

## D
dung beetles, 25–27

## E
Egyptian vulture, 5–6
elephants, 11, 17–18

## F
fiber, 9, 14, 20

## G
gorillas, 19–20

## K
koalas, 10–11

## M
moths, 20–21

## N
nutrients, 6–7, 14, 18–21, 26

## P
pandas, 9–10
predators, 23–24

## R
rabbits, 14, 20

## T
termites, 12–13

## W
warthogs, 17–18
wolves, 24